reflect.

reflect.

A self-reflective journal with mindful prompts & poems

By Tiana DeNicola & Sophie Dunne
from *shifting her experience*

Even as a couple, we know that the most important relationship you'll ever have is the one with yourself. We created this self-reflective journal as a tool for discovering who you are and to improve your own self-awareness. We were inspired by our motivated listeners from our podcast, *she.* by *shifting her experience*, who always stay curious.

The best way and the only way to fill out this journal is to be completely honest with yourself — there are no right or wrong answers. We purposely did not include dates in this journal because there are no deadlines. Go at your own pace, this is all about you.

Conversations with yourself are an essential process in the evolution of you.

Tiana & Sophie

I know people's traits, their characters, and quirks
My perception of their makeup and how it all works
But what are my observations of my own person?
Who am I to me that makes me so certain?

Table of Contents

For self-discovery

My life experiences cause me to question
The life I live until I'm done
But when it comes time to ponder
Who is the person that I've become?

When I think of who I am, what words come to mind? Circle all words that apply.

Easygoing   Patient   Honest   Resourceful

Adventurous   Genuine   Independent

Adaptable   Kind   Loyal   Fearless

Enthusiastic   Practical   Witty

Passionate   Disciplined   Humble   Gentle

Hard-working   Happy   Affectionate

A few other words that describe me:

_____

_____

_____

_____

_____

Why did I circle those words? What qualities in myself from the words that I circled, do I admire most?

_____

_____

_____

_____

_____

_____

_____

_____

_____

_____

_____

_____

Are there any qualities that I want to improve on?

_____

_____

_____

_____

_____

Are there any personal development areas that I'd like to improve on? Check any that apply.

☐ Emotional ☐ Physical ☐ Spiritual

☐ Career ☐ Relationships ☐ Wellbeing

☐ Confidence ☐ Communication ☐ Motivation

Why are these areas important to me?

_____

_____

_____

_____

_____

_____

_____

_____

_____

_____

_____

_____

What can I do now to start improving on these areas that I checked?

_____

_____

_____

_____

_____

_____

_____

_____

_____

_____

_____

_____

_____

_____

_____

_____

_____

_____

Journaling and self-reflection are great methods for improving self-awareness.
***Why* do I want to improve my self-awareness?**

☐ To improve my decision-making

☐ To help manage my emotions

☐ To boost my productivity

☐ To boost my self-esteem

☐ To strengthen my relationships

☐ To make a positive change

☐ To get in touch with my wants/needs

☐ To become the best version of myself

Do the areas I checked benefit me or others?

_____

_____

_____

_____

_____

_____

_____

What are 5 things I'm really good at?

(1)

(2)

(3)

(4)

(5)

What are 5 accomplishments I'm proud of?

(1)

(2)

(3)

(4)

(5)

Why did I write down those accomplishments?
Why am I proud of them?

_____

_____

_____

_____

_____

_____

_____

_____

_____

_____

_____

_____

_____

_____

_____

_____

_____

_____

Do I see any resemblance in the things I'm good at versus the things I've accomplished?

Yes!   No   I'm not sure

Do my accomplishments indicate what I value?

Yes!   No   I'm not sure

What are some things I value in life?

_____

_____

_____

_____

_____

_____

_____

_____

_____

_____

_____

_____

_____

I really want to reflect on who I am. I'm going to look at each statement and circle the number I feel best represents my feelings:

0 = Not me   **1** = Rarely me   **2** = Sometimes me
3 = I'm not sure   **4** = Most likely me
5 = Definitely me

I am comfortable making mistakes

0   1   2   3   4   5

I'm able to put my emotions aside when dealing with issues

0   1   2   3   4   5

I created the life I am living

0   1   2   3   4   5

I feel comfortable sitting in silence in most scenarios

0   1   2   3   4   5

I'm always in search for deeper meanings

0   1   2   3   4   5

I know what is most important to me in life

0   1   2   3   4   5

I know my strengths and weaknesses

0   1   2   3   4   5

I prefer to avoid conflict or confrontation

0   1   2   3   4   5

It's important to me to be unique

0   1   2   3   4   5

I don't let my fears influence my decisions

0   1   2   3   4   5

I have outlined my goals and ambitions

0   1   2   3   4   5

I can describe my ideal work environment

0   1   2   3   4   5

I can usually predict how I will react in a situation

0   1   2   3   4   5

I get upset when things don't go my way

0   1   2   3   4   5

I tend to second-guess myself

0   1   2   3   4   5

When I look at my answers to the previous exercise, what do I notice about myself? What prompts did I give myself a 5 in? What prompts did I give myself a 0?

_____

_____

_____

_____

_____

_____

_____

_____

_____

_____

_____

_____

_____

_____

_____

_____

_____

_____

Write down 5 adjectives that describe me:

(1)

(2)

(3)

(4)

(5)

Write down 5 emotions that describe me:

(1)

(2)

(3)

(4)

(5)

Fill in the blanks:

An emotion I'd like to feel more of is _____

I'm truly happy when _____

I wish I could be more _____

Success to me is _____

My greatest strength is _____

I feel most relaxed when _____

I feel fulfilled when _____

I notice my confidence going up when _____

I would describe my energy as _____

An emotion I often conceal is _____

When I look at the blanks I filled in, is there a pattern I see in how I view myself or view the world around me?

_____

_____

_____

_____

_____

_____

_____

_____

_____

_____

_____

_____

_____

_____

In one word, describe how I feel about myself at this moment.

_____

Would I rather?

Lead	Listen
Think	Feel
Inspire	Advocate
Teach	Learn
Explore	Examine
Talk	Write
Daydream	Reflect
Intellect	Wisdom
Adventure	Stability
Compete	Support

How do I feel about anger?
Circle the words that I feel define anger for me.

Justifiable   Cathartic   Necessary   Unnecessary

Scary   Appropriate   Inappropriate

Healthy   Reflective   Motivating   Irrational

Positive   Negative   Loss of control

Hostile   Frustrating   Immature   Avoidable

Why do I feel this way?

_____

_____

_____

_____

_____

_____

_____

_____

_____

_____

_____

_____

True or False?

I laugh daily

True   False

I feel like I am reaching my full potential

True   False

I have goals and ambitions for the future

True   False

I check in with myself daily

True   False

I am ambitious

True   False

I am inspired by the world around me to be a better person

True   False

I feel that I maintain a balanced life

True   False

When I look at my answers in the true or false exercise, is there anything in particular that I notice about myself? If I answered false to any of them, why did I do so?

_____
_____
_____
_____
_____
_____
_____
_____
_____
_____
_____
_____
_____
_____
_____
_____
_____
_____
_____

Who, what, and where makes me feel good?

_____

_____

_____

_____

_____

_____

_____

_____

_____

_____

What do I struggle with?

_____

_____

_____

_____

_____

_____

_____

_____

_____

On a scale from 1-5, 5 being the highest, how would I rate these in regards to their importance to me?

Self-development ◯

Intimacy ◯

Relationships ◯

Creativity ◯

Education ◯

Adventure ◯

Communication ◯

Trust ◯

Vulnerability ◯

Doodle something! Anything, really.

Why did I doodle that?

_____

_____

_____

_____

_____

_____

_____

_____

Is there a story behind this doodle?

_____

_____

_____

_____

_____

_____

_____

_____

_____

_____

_____

For the past

Evolutionary-changes blossom my being
I see its shapes from then and now
But with what inspiration did the sculptures shape me?
Who was it that helped, when, and how?

Past and present

What types of things did I enjoy doing as a child?

Do I do anything today that has similar qualities?

Is there a time in my life that I want to do-over? Why did I pick this?

_____

_____

_____

_____

_____

_____

_____

_____

_____

_____

_____

_____

_____

_____

_____

_____

_____

_____

_____

_____

What do I believe has been my biggest mistake so far in life? What did I learn from it?

_____

_____

_____

_____

_____

_____

_____

_____

_____

_____

_____

_____

_____

_____

_____

_____

_____

_____

_____

Check the words that apply to me.
I usually protect myself in life by:

☐ Setting up boundaries

☐ Asking for advice

☐ Following my own advice

☐ Being transparent with who I am

☐ Having an alter ego

☐ Masking who I am

☐ Communicating my concerns

☐ Writing my concerns down

☐ Finding healthy distractions

☐ Establishing a support network

☐ Avoiding negativity

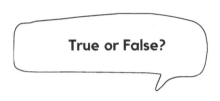

True or False?

I am proud of my past and how far I've come

True   False

I believe in giving people second chances

True   False

**My personality is similar now to how it was
when I was younger**

True   False

**I feel comfortable making decisions even if others
disagree with them**

True   False

**In the past, I have treated someone in a way
that I regret**

True   False

I rarely dwell on my regrets

True   False

When I look at my answers in the true or false exercise, is there anything in particular that I notice about myself? If I answered false to any of them, why did I do so?

_____

_____

_____

_____

_____

_____

_____

_____

_____

_____

_____

_____

_____

_____

_____

_____

_____

_____

When I was younger, did I ever think of *who* I wanted to be, or did I only ever think of *what* I wanted to be and have in life?

_____

_____

_____

_____

_____

_____

_____

_____

_____

_____

_____

_____

_____

_____

_____

_____

_____

_____

_____

_____

What event from my past would I most want to see a recording of?

_____

_____

_____

_____

_____

_____

_____

_____

_____

_____

_____

_____

_____

_____

_____

_____

_____

_____

_____

_____

What limiting beliefs am I holding on to?

_____

_____

_____

_____

_____

_____

_____

_____

_____

_____

_____

_____

_____

_____

_____

_____

_____

_____

_____

_____

What do I enjoy doing regardless of other people's opinions?

_____

_____

_____

_____

_____

_____

_____

_____

_____

_____

_____

_____

_____

_____

_____

_____

_____

_____

_____

For relationships

With everyone I know, I've once been a stranger
Building bonds that put my nature on show
And you help cushion me through pleasure and danger
But I'll never know me like you know.

I'm going to think about my friendships for a moment. What do I value in a friendship? Circle 5 traits that are most important to me.

Loyal   Humorous   Inspirational   Witty

Dependable   Empathetic   Honest

Kind   Protective   Nurturing   Creative

Intellectual   Adventurous   Encouraging

Available   Attentive   Caring   Opinionated

Non-judgmental   Entertaining   Forgiving

Comforting   Invested   Considerate   Playful

Enjoyable   Motivational   Boisterous

Flexibile   Interested   Inclusive   Spiritual

other: _____

What kind of friend am I to others?
Circle 5 traits that I bring to the relationship.

Loyal   Humorous   Inspirational   Witty

Dependable   Empathetic   Honest

Kind   Protective   Nurturing   Creative

Intellectual   Adventurous   Encouraging

Available   Attentive   Caring   Opinionated

Non-judgmental   Entertaining   Forgiving

Comforting   Invested   Considerate   Playful

Enjoyable   Motivational   Boisterous

Flexibile   Interested   Inclusive   Spiritual

other: _____

What type of people do I enjoy spending time with? (Intelligent, open-minded, adventurous, opinionated, quiet, funny, etc.) Why?

_____

_____

_____

_____

_____

_____

_____

_____

_____

_____

_____

Do I seek out people who are similar or different from me? Why is that?

_____

_____

_____

_____

Fill in the blanks:

A genuine friend is someone who_____

My friends say I am_____

I'd say I am_____

When I'm with people I want them to feel_____

I'm the go-to person if my friend wants to_____

I'd describe my closest friends as_____

I can always be myself around_____

Life would be boring without_____

I feel at peace when_____

Something that feels like home is_____

True or False?

I can rely on my friends for support

True   False

My friends can rely on me for support

True   False

I randomly check in with my friends

True   False

I often spend my time helping others

True   False

I have people in my life that inspire me

True   False

I feel that I am a good listener

True   False

I have friends that fulfill different parts of my life

True   False

When I look at my answers in the true or false exercise, is there anything in particular that I notice about myself? If I answered false to any of them, why did I do so?

_____

_____

_____

_____

_____

_____

_____

_____

_____

_____

_____

_____

_____

_____

_____

_____

_____

When it comes to romantic relationships, what do I look for in someone?

_____

_____

_____

_____

_____

_____

_____

_____

_____

Are there any deal-breakers for me when it comes to relationships?

_____

_____

_____

_____

_____

_____

_____

_____

_____

Describe what a partner who is my equal would act like? What does it mean to me to be with someone who is my equal?

_____

_____

_____

_____

_____

_____

_____

_____

_____

_____

_____

_____

_____

_____

_____

_____

_____

_____

_____

_____

What is *my* definition of love?
What does love look like?
How do I want to be loved?

_____

_____

_____

_____

_____

_____

_____

_____

_____

_____

_____

_____

_____

_____

_____

_____

_____

_____

_____

Do I judge the people in my life by their intentions or by their actions?

_____

_____

_____

_____

_____

_____

_____

_____

_____

_____

Do I judge myself in life by my intentions or by my actions?

_____

_____

_____

_____

_____

_____

_____

I really want to reflect on what's important to me in relationships. I'm going to look at each statement and circle the number I feel best represents my feelings:

0 = Not me   **1** = Rarely me   **2** = Sometimes me
3 = I'm not sure   **4** = Most likely me
5 = Definitely me

I find it easy to trust people I'm in relationships with

0   1   2   3   4   5

I trust my judgment when letting new people into my life

0   1   2   3   4   5

I prefer to date someone similar to me

0   1   2   3   4   5

Equality is very important to me in both romantic and platonic relationships

0   1   2   3   4   5

I find it challenging to read others' emotions

0   1   2   3   4   5

People often end up letting me down

0   1   2   3   4   5

I treat others better than I treat myself

0   1   2   3   4   5

I would consider my close friends as family

0   1   2   3   4   5

When interacting with people, I examine how they respond to me

0   1   2   3   4   5

People tell me that I'm a positive person

0   1   2   3   4   5

In an argument, I can usually see the other person's point of view

0   1   2   3   4   5

I enjoy meeting new people

0   1   2   3   4   5

I'm easy for people to get to know

0   1   2   3   4   5

I often overshare in conversations with people

0   1   2   3   4   5

Social interaction is instrumental to my happiness

0   1   2   3   4   5

When I look at my answers to the previous exercise, what do I notice about myself? What prompts did I give myself a 5 in? What prompts did I give myself a 0?

_____

_____

_____

_____

_____

_____

_____

_____

_____

_____

_____

_____

_____

_____

_____

_____

_____

_____

_____

Can I remember a time that I laughed so hard it hurt? Who was I with? What were we doing?

_____

_____

_____

_____

_____

_____

_____

_____

_____

_____

_____

_____

_____

_____

_____

_____

_____

_____

Someone comes to me to apologize.
How would I like to receive the apology?
Check all that apply.

☐ Acknowledgment of hurtful actions

☐ An explanation

☐ Follow through with actions

☐ Accept responsibility for actions

☐ Express regret or remorse

☐ Request forgiveness

Why?

_____

_____

_____

_____

_____

_____

_____

_____

_____

_____

What is my process of apologizing? What stages do I follow when apologizing to someone?

_____

_____

_____

_____

_____

_____

_____

_____

_____

_____

_____

_____

_____

_____

_____

_____

_____

_____

_____

There are 4 different communication styles.

Passive
Passive-aggressive
Aggressive
Assertive

Which one(s) am I?
How do I usually communicate with people?

_____

_____

_____

_____

_____

_____

_____

_____

_____

_____

_____

_____

_____

_____

What factors are important to me in order to be taken seriously by people?

Emotional Intelligence is defined as the understanding of human emotions—your own and other people's. It's the capacity to be aware of, control, and express emotions as well as handling interpersonal relationships accordingly.

How would I rate my Emotional Intelligence? Where would I fall on this scale?

could be
better

the best
it's been!

Why?

_____

_____

_____

_____

_____

_____

_____

_____

Emotional Maturity is defined as how well you are able to respond to situations, control your emotions, and behave in an appropriate manner. It refers to a higher state of self-awareness where we're guided by our senses and intuition. Emotional Intelligence is the understanding of emotions, whereas Emotional Maturity is the application of that knowledge.

How would I rate my Emotional Maturity? Where would I fall on this scale?

could be better

the best it's been!

Why?

_____

_____

_____

_____

_____

_____

_____

Write about a time in my life that comes to mind when I think of the word *affection?*

_____

_____

_____

_____

_____

_____

_____

_____

_____

_____

_____

_____

_____

_____

_____

_____

_____

_____

_____

Write about a time in my life that comes to mind when I think of the word *solidarity?*

For self-love

Like the wilting flower
We all have our moments
Nature is inevitable and so is our wilt.
We don't taunt the flower when it passes through stages
Yet we insult our process and its natural tilt.

What are 5 things I like about myself?

(1)

(2)

(3)

(4)

(5)

When I think about self-love, what's important to me?

_____

_____

_____

_____

_____

_____

_____

_____

_____

Do I have a habit that soothes or calms me?

True or False?

I feel in control of my life

True   False

I feel at peace in regards to my past

True   False

I am passionate about something

True   False

I would consider myself a spiritual person

True   False

I find it easy to love myself

True   False

I regularly make time for self-reflection

True   False

I regularly make time for self-care

True   False

When I look at my answers in the true or false exercise, is there anything in particular that I notice about myself? If I answered false to any of them, why did I do so?

_____

_____

_____

_____

_____

_____

_____

_____

_____

_____

_____

_____

_____

_____

_____

_____

_____

_____

_____

_____

Arrange these words from most to least important to me:

Companionship   Love   Achievement

Self-respect   Fulfillment   Independence

Relaxation   Wellness   Education

Financial stability   Passion   Spirituality

_____

_____

_____

_____

_____

_____

_____

_____

_____

_____

_____

_____

When was the last time I asked myself,
"How are you?"

_____

_____

_____

_____

_____

_____

_____

_____

_____

_____

When was the last time I asked myself,
"Are you happy?"

_____

_____

_____

_____

_____

_____

_____

Is there a word or phrase to describe me that society thinks is a weakness but I see as a strength?

_____

_____

_____

_____

_____

_____

_____

_____

_____

_____

Why is this a strength in my eyes?

_____

_____

_____

_____

_____

_____

_____

Can I remember a time where I concealed an emotion? Maybe I held back tears or masked my true feelings towards someone or something. Why did I camouflage that emotion?

_____

_____

_____

_____

_____

_____

_____

_____

_____

_____

_____

_____

_____

_____

_____

_____

_____

How do I express affection to others?

_____

_____

_____

_____

_____

_____

_____

_____

_____

How would I like to have affection reciprocated?

_____

_____

_____

_____

_____

_____

_____

_____

How do I feel about crying?

_____

_____

_____

_____

_____

_____

_____

_____

_____

_____

_____

_____

_____

_____

_____

_____

_____

_____

Draw a picture of myself.

In the picture I drew of myself, am I happy?

_____

Why or why not?

_____

_____

_____

So, what makes me happy?

_____

_____

_____

_____

_____

_____

_____

_____

_____

_____

_____

_____

_____

Draw a picture of what "me time" looks like.

How often do I set aside time for myself?

_____

What activities or lack thereof, do I consider a part of "me time"?

_____

_____

_____

_____

_____

_____

_____

_____

_____

_____

_____

_____

_____

_____

_____

_____

_____

_____

For the hypothetical

A meet, a greet, a laugh, a cry
An argument, an apology, a walk-away, a lie
I do what I have to when protecting my survival
The essential strategy as part of my revival.

Scenario 1:
If a friend was to describe me to someone who has never met me before, what would I want them to say about me?

_____

_____

_____

_____

_____

_____

_____

_____

_____

_____

_____

_____

_____

_____

_____

_____

_____

_____

Scenario 2:
A friend or family member confides in me about something going on in their life. When they're talking, am I listening to give advice or am I listening to understand?

_____

_____

_____

_____

_____

_____

_____

_____

_____

If I'm listening to understand instead of listening to answer, otherwise known as active listening, which of these do I find easy to do?

Pay attention   Make eye contact   Encourage

Use facial expressions   Have an open body posture

Ask questions   Respect   Provide feedback

Defer judgment   Not interrupt

Scenario 3:
My friend comes to me and tells me that something I had said the day before hurt their feelings. What is my initial reaction?

_____

_____

_____

_____

_____

_____

_____

_____

_____

_____

_____

_____

_____

_____

_____

_____

Is this scenario something I feel that I can take accountability for?

Yes   No   I'm not sure

Scenario 4:
Yesterday, a friend said something to me that hurt my feelings. I want to talk to them about it. What do I say?

_____

_____

_____

_____

_____

_____

_____

_____

_____

_____

_____

_____

_____

_____

_____

_____

_____

_____

Scenario 5:
I receive feedback on a project I completed. The feedback doesn't align with how I feel about my work. Do I take it personally or do I see this as constructive guidance? Why?

_____

_____

_____

_____

_____

_____

_____

_____

_____

_____

_____

_____

_____

_____

_____

_____

_____

Scenario 6:
I want to speak to my boss about a promotion that I believe I deserve. How am I feeling before I meet with them?
Circle some words that resonate with me.

Doubtful	Confident	Annoyed
Eager	Nervous	Overwhelmed
Insecure	Deserving	Undeserving
Cautious	Frantic	Powerful
Pensive	Breathless	Excited
Calm	Agreeable	Defensive

Is this a recurring pattern for me when I have to ask for things?

_____

_____

_____

_____

_____

_____

Scenario 7:

If I was in someone else's body for a day, how would I talk about myself to others? How would I want others to perceive me?

_____

_____

_____

_____

_____

_____

_____

_____

_____

_____

_____

_____

_____

_____

_____

_____

_____

_____

Scenario 8:

**Someone I really care about let me down.
What is my reaction? Feel free to circle some words
to get started.**

Frustrated	Defeated	Disappointed
Logical	Deceived	Confrontational
Understanding	Angry	Self-critical

_____

_____

_____

_____

_____

_____

_____

_____

_____

_____

_____

_____

_____

_____

_____

Scenario 9:
A stranger cuts in front of me in line.
What do I do, if anything?

_____

_____

_____

_____

_____

_____

_____

Is it easier for me to be assertive with
strangers than it is with people in my
personal life? Why?

_____

_____

_____

_____

_____

_____

_____

_____

Scenario 10:

I'm speaking to someone who isn't understanding or trying to understand my point of view. How do I react or deal with the situation?

_____

_____

_____

_____

_____

_____

_____

_____

_____

_____

_____

_____

_____

_____

_____

_____

_____

_____

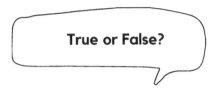

True or False?

I find it easy to ask for what I want

True   False

I feel in control of my reactions regardless of the situation

True   False

Certain environments lower my self-esteem

True   False

Most of my fears are based on reality

True   False

Before I make a decision, I always consider every possible outcome

True   False

I don't usually let people influence my decisions

True   False

I spend time worrying about scenarios that haven't actually happened

True   False

When I look at my answers in the true or false exercise, is there anything in particular that I notice about myself? If I answered false to any of them, why did I do so?

_____

_____

_____

_____

_____

_____

_____

_____

_____

_____

_____

_____

_____

_____

_____

_____

_____

_____

For inspiration

A honey bee is small in comparison to me
"But do you know your significance, tiny little bee?"
My environment, its existence, its progression, and health
Relies on you and your resourceful wealth
Yet we overlook your influence and your relationship to me
"You don't realize how much you do for us, significant little bee."

True or False?

I am often able to inspire myself

True   False

My environment inspires me

True   False

People in my life inspire me

True   False

Relaxation is an integral part of feeling inspired

True   False

I feel inspired on a daily basis

True   False

I can draw inspiration from little things

True   False

I feel most inspired when I'm alone

True   False

When I look at my answers in the true or false exercise, is there anything in particular that I notice about myself? If I answered false to any of them, why did I do so?

_____

_____

_____

_____

_____

_____

_____

_____

_____

_____

_____

_____

_____

_____

_____

_____

_____

_____

_____

What inspires me?
Feel free to write all over the page.

What did I hear recently that inspired me?

When was the last time somebody did me a favor?

_____

_____

_____

_____

_____

_____

_____

_____

When was the last time I did someone a favor?

_____

_____

_____

_____

_____

_____

_____

_____

_____

If I could do 5 things without any limitations, what would I do?

_____

_____

_____

_____

_____

_____

_____

_____

_____

_____

_____

_____

_____

_____

_____

_____

_____

_____

_____

What's something interesting that I learned recently? Can I think of a few things?

_____

_____

_____

_____

_____

_____

_____

_____

_____

_____

_____

_____

_____

_____

_____

_____

_____

Is there something I see in myself that I want others to see more of?

_____

_____

_____

_____

_____

_____

_____

_____

_____

_____

_____

_____

_____

_____

_____

_____

_____

_____

_____

Who in my life has had the biggest impact on me?

_____

_____

_____

_____

_____

_____

_____

_____

_____

_____

_____

_____

_____

_____

_____

_____

_____

_____

_____

_____

_____

What am I capable of achieving?

_____

_____

_____

_____

_____

_____

_____

_____

_____

What does it mean to live a good life?

_____

_____

_____

_____

_____

_____

_____

_____

_____

_____

What makes me feel productive?
Circle what applies to me.

Doing physical activities   Reading   Setting goals

Using my imagination   Journaling   Meditating

Meal planning   Ticking off lists   Meeting friends

Creating mood boards   Creating vision boards

Taking a bath   Creating something   Relaxing

Listening to music   Looking at old pictures

Seeking out new opportunities   Creating a budget

Learning something new   Being in nature

Getting dressed up   Doing tasks in the moment

Traveling   Sitting in the sunlight   Being organized

Having a meaningful conversation

Maintaining low stress levels   Tidying up

Why did I circle these?
Why do these examples make me feel productive?

_____

_____

_____

_____

_____

_____

_____

_____

_____

_____

_____

_____

_____

_____

_____

_____

_____

_____

_____

_____

I'm going to do a word association exercise. When I think of these words, what's the first thing that comes to mind?

Love = _____

Success = _____

Achievement = _____

Security = _____

Power = _____

Guilt = _____

Gratitude = _____

Respect = _____

Health = _____

I'm going to use this page to write down a to-do list of goals for myself, with no deadlines.

☐ _____

☐ _____

☐ _____

☐ _____

☐ _____

☐ _____

☐ _____

☐ _____

☐ _____

☐ _____

For the future me

I take the canvas and position it neatly
Catching the light and the view ahead.
I splash the paint from corner to corner
With visions of what I want versus what comes out instead.
The paint is vibrant and full of fire
And I feel the thrill of it, my mood growing higher.
But I decide to slow down and breathe it all in
So I can savor this moment before I let the next one begin.

When I think of where I want my life to go, what are some feelings I have towards it? Circle all that apply.

Optimistic	Hopeful	Troubled
Pressured	Curious	Excited
Overwhelmed	Thankful	Distracted
Confused	Confident	Worried

Why did I circle these? What's contributing to these feelings?

_____

_____

_____

_____

_____

_____

_____

_____

_____

_____

_____

What are some emotions that I express daily? What usually triggers these emotions?

_____

_____

_____

_____

_____

_____

_____

_____

_____

_____

_____

_____

_____

_____

_____

_____

_____

_____

_____

_____

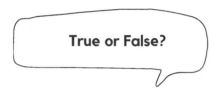

True or False?

I am excited about my future

True   False

I would like to live in the moment more

True   False

There is someone in my life whose footsteps I'd like to follow in

True   False

I am more focused on relationships than goals

True   False

I embrace new experiences enthusiastically

True   False

I spend a lot of time daydreaming about my future

True   False

I have a sense of what my purpose is

True   False

When I look at my answers in the true or false exercise, is there anything in particular that I notice about myself? If I answered false to any of them, why did I do so?

_____

_____

_____

_____

_____

_____

_____

_____

_____

_____

_____

_____

_____

_____

_____

_____

_____

_____

When I look back, what are the 5 most significant events in my life? Why do I feel like they are significant?

(1)

(2)

(3)

(4)

(5)

Is there something I feel like I have to do that I haven't done yet? What is it and why?

_____

_____

_____

_____

_____

_____

_____

_____

What would happen if I never got it done? Would I still be happy?

_____

_____

_____

_____

_____

_____

_____

_____

_____

I really want to explore the present and my future. I'm going to look at each statement and circle the number I feel best represents my feelings:

0 = Not me   1 = Rarely me   2 = Sometimes me
3 = I'm not sure   4 = Most likely me
5 = Definitely me

I like to visualize my future before setting goals

0   1   2   3   4   5

I'm confident in my ability to achieve the goals I set

0   1   2   3   4   5

I enjoy breaking out of tradition

0   1   2   3   4   5

I prefer to live in the moment rather than think about my future

0   1   2   3   4   5

I'm quite hard on myself

0   1   2   3   4   5

I only take calculated risks

0   1   2   3   4   5

I stay true to my values regardless of the situation

0   1   2   3   4   5

My social circle influences my life positively

0   1   2   3   4   5

I care more about how my life feels rather than how it looks

0   1   2   3   4   5

I believe technology gets in the way of my happiness

0   1   2   3   4   5

I am very affectionate with people I care about

0   1   2   3   4   5

I prefer to let my emotions guide me

0   1   2   3   4   5

I am more of a big-picture person

0   1   2   3   4   5

I know where I want to be in 5 years

0   1   2   3   4   5

I know where I want to be in 10 years

0   1   2   3   4   5

I am living my life to the fullest

0   1   2   3   4   5

When I look at my answers to the exercise, what do I notice about myself? What prompts did I give myself a 5 in? What prompts did I give myself a 0?

_____

_____

_____

_____

_____

_____

_____

_____

_____

_____

_____

_____

_____

_____

_____

_____

_____

_____

What do I believe holds people back?

_____

_____

_____

_____

_____

_____

_____

_____

_____

Is there something holding me back?

_____

_____

_____

_____

_____

_____

_____

_____

_____

What are some goals that I have?
Feel free to write all over the page.

What are the traits I want my future self to have?
How would I describe my future self?
What do I act like, think, or embody?

_____

_____

_____

_____

_____

_____

_____

_____

_____

_____

_____

_____

_____

_____

_____

_____

_____

_____

_____

_____

_____

**When I think about my life, both past and present,
what do I feel I am meant to do on this earth?
Is there something that I feel is my greater purpose?**
This could be as simple as, "to learn," "to teach,"
"to love..."

When I look back on what I've written and discovered in this self-reflective journal, what have I learned about myself? Did anything surprise me?

_____

_____

_____

_____

_____

_____

_____

_____

_____

_____

_____

_____

_____

_____

_____

_____

_____

_____

Is there anything else I want to say?
Is there anything I want to outline?

Still breathing
Still beating
Reflect
Respect.

13222025R00080